Anonymous

Acts of Incorporation and By-Laws of the New Westminster Board of Trade,

New Westminster, B.C., 1883

Anonymous

Acts of Incorporation and By-Laws of the New Westminster Board of Trade,
New Westminster, B.C., 1883

ISBN/EAN: 9783744794008

Printed in Europe, USA, Canada, Australia, Japan

Cover: Foto ©Suzi / pixelio.de

More available books at **www.hansebooks.com**

ACTS OF INCORPORATION

—AND—

BY·LAWS

—OF THE—

NEW WESTMINSTER

BOARD OF TRADE

New Westminster, B.C., 1883.

ADOPTED AT THE QUARTERLY GENERAL MEETING 22ND FEBRUARY, AND ADJOURNED MEETING 28TH FEBRUARY, 1883.

NEW WESTMINSTER:

BRITISH COLUMBIAN NEWSPAPER AND JOB PRINTING OFFICE,

1883.

OFFICERS.

1883-1884.

EBENEZER BROWN, - - - - - - - - - PRESIDENT.
JAMES CUNNINGHAM, - - - - - - VICE-PRESIDENT.
THOMAS J. TRAPP, - - - - - - - - - SECRETARY.

COUNCIL. (8)

G. C. MAJOR,
JOHN HENDRY,
J. A. WEBSTER,
A. EWEN,
ROBT. DICKINSON,
JAMES WISE,
S. TRAPP,
H. V. EDMONDS.

ARBITRATION BOARD. (12)

C. G. MAJOR,
JOHN HENDRY,
J. A. WEBSTER,
A. EWEN,
ROBT. DICKINSON,
JAMES WISE,
S. TRAPP,
H. V. EDMONDS,
W. McCOLL,
C. McDONOUGH,
WM. RAE,
A. HASLAM.

156444

LIST OF MEMBERS.

ADAIR, WILLIAM, B.
ADAIR, JOHN, Jr.
BROWN, EBENEZER.
BLACKIE, WALTER.
CUNNINGHAM, JAMES.
CHISHOLM, DONALD.
DODD, WM.
DOUGLAS, BENJAMIN.
DEANE, R. W.
DICKINSON, ROBERT.
ENGLISH, MARSHALL M.
EDMONDS, HENRY V.
EWEN, ALEXANDER.
ELLIOTT, HENRY.
EICKHOFF, FREDRICK.
FISHER, ISAAC B.
FRASER, ANGUS C.
HOMER, JOSHUA A. R.
HASLAM, ANDREW.
HENDRY, JOHN.
HARVEY, JAMES W.
HERRING, ARTHUR M.
KEARY, W. H.
LEISER, GUSTAV.
LAIDLAW, JAMES A.
LADNER, THOMAS E.
MAJOR, CHARLES G.
McCOLL, WILLIAM.
McNAIR, DAVID.
McNEELY, THOMAS.
McDONOUGH, CHARLES.
ONDERDONK, ANDREW.
PLEACE, JOHN H.
PEARSON, THOMAS R.
ROUSSEAU, JAMES.
ROBSON, JNO.
RAE, WILLIAM.
SCOULLAR, EDWIN S.
TRAPP, SAMUEL.
TRAPP, THOMAS JNO.
THOMAS, ROBERT.
TIFFIN, JOHN B.
WEBSTER, JOHN A.
WILLIE, LOUIS.
WISE, JAMES.
WEBSTER, GEO. C.

To the Honorable, the Secretary of State for the Dominion of Canada:—Know all men by these presents, that we, the several persons whose signatures and seals are hereto subscribed and set, and whose occupations, respectively, are those set opposite our respective signatures, do hereby associate ourselves together as a Board of Trade, under the provisions of the Act of Parliament of Canada, 37 Vic., (1874), Chap. 51, as amended by the Act 39 Vic., (1876), Chap. 34; and we do hereby appoint Henry Valentine Edmonds as Secretary to the said Board of Trade; and we do hereby specify the name assumed by the Association, and by which it shall be known, to be "THE NEW WESTMINSTER BOARD OF TRADE," and the name of the District in which the same is situate, and its business transacted to be New Westminster, and the name of the person so elected Secretary to be Henry Valentine Edmonds.

Witness our hands and seals.

Dated the 10th day of October, A.D. one thousand eight hundred and eighty-two.

SIGNATURES.	OCCUPATION.	WITNESS.
Joshua A. R. Homer	Merchant	Charles E. Woods
James Cunningham	Merchant	Charles E. Woods
Ebenezer Brown	Merchant	Charles E. Woods
Charles G. Major	Merchaut	Charles E. Woods
James W. Harvey	Merchant	Charles E. Woods
Gustav Leiser	Merchant	Charles E. Woods
James A. Laidlaw	Salmon Canner	Charles E. Woods
Samuel Trapp	Merchant	Charles E. Woods
Thomas Jno. Trapp	Merchant	Charles E. Woods
Charles McDonough	Merchant	Charles E. Woods
James Wise	Merchant	Charles E. Woods
Geo. C. Webster	Mill Owner	Charles E. Woods
Thomas R. Pearson	Merchant	Charles E. Woods
Jno. Robson	Merchant	Charles E. Woods
Edwin S. Scoullar	Merchant	Charles E. Woods
Robert Dickinson	Merchant	Charles E. Woods
William McColl	Merchant	Charles E. Woods
Isaac B. Fisher	Banker	Charles E. Woods
John H. Pleace	Merchant	Charles E. Woods
Arthur M. Herring	Druggist	Charles E. Woods
William Rae	Merchant	Charles E. Woods
Robert Thomas	Merchant	Charles E. Woods
Louis Willie	Merchant	Charles E. Woods
John Hendry	Mill Owner	Charles E. Woods
Henry Elliott	Merchant	Charles E. Woods
Fredrick Eickhoff	Merchant	Charles E. Woods
Andrew Haslam	Mill Owner	Charles E. Woods
David McNair	Mill Owner	Charles E. Woods
Walter Blackie	Blacksmith	Charles E. Woods
Donald Chisholm	Merchant	Charles E. Woods
Marshall M. English	Merchant	Charles E. Woods
Henry V. Edmonds	Auctioneer	Charles E. Woods
Alexander Ewen	Fish Monger	Charles E. Woods
W. H. Keary	Merchant	Charles E. Woods
James Rousseau	Merchant	Charles E. Woods
R. W. Deane	Broker	Charles E. Woods
John A. Webster	Mill Owner	Charles E. Woods
William B. Adair	Prop. Salmon Cannery	Charles E. Woods
Angus C. Fraser	Lumberman	Charles E. Woods
John B. Tiffin	Manufacturer	Charles E. Woods
Thomas McNeely	Merchant	Charles E. Woods
Thomas E. Ladner	Salmon Canner	Charles E. Woods
John Adair, Jr	Salmon Canner	Charles E. Woods
Benjamin Douglas	Saddler	Charles E. Woods
Andrew Onderdonk	Civil Eng'r & Contract'r	E. A. Cunningham
Wm. Dodd	Express Agent	O. R. Warwick

I, Charles Edwards Woods, of New Westminster, British Columbia, do hereby acknowledge and declare that the above certificate was signed and sealed by the respective persons by whom it purports to have been signed and sealed, in my presence, with the exception of the names Andrew Onderdonk, and Wm. Dodd, William B. Adair, Angus C. Fraser, Thomas McNeely, Thomas E. Ladner and John Adair Jr. **CHARLES E. WOODS.**

Taken and acknowledged before me, at New Westminster, this twelfth day of December, A. D. 1882.

GORDON E. CORBOULD, [Seal.]
Notary Public.

I, Henry Valentine Edmonds, of the city of New Westminster, in the Province of British Columbia, Secretary of the New Westminster Board of Trade, do hereby acknowledge and declare that the hereto annexed certificate was signed and sealed by the respective persons by whom it purports to have been signed and sealed ; that the respective occupations set opposite the respective names of such persons are their true occupations respectively, and the said persons reside within the judicial district of New Westminster. **HENRY V. EDMONDS.**

Taken and acknowledged before me at New Westminster, this twelfth day of December, A. D. 1882.

GORDON E. CORBOULD, [Seal.]
Notary Public, British Columbia.

DEPARTMENT OF THE SECRETARY OF STATE OF CANADA,
REGISTRAR'S BRANCH, Ottawa, 17th, January, 1883. }

I do hereby certify that the foregoing is a true and correct copy of a certificate purporting to be made under the provisions of the 39th Victoria, Chap. 34, Sections 2 and 3, intituled, "An Act to amend the 37th Vic., Chap. 51, intituled, 'An Act to authorize the incorporation of Boards of Trade in the Dominion,'" for incorporation of "The New Westminster Board of Trade," and recorded in the Registrar's Branch of the Department of the Secretary of State for Canada, on the 17th day of January, 1883, in lib. 28, folio 50. **HECTOR L. LANGEVIN,**
For Secretary of State and Registrar-General of Canada.

The New Westminster Board of Trade is incorporated under the following Acts of Parliament of the Dominion of Canada, viz.: 37-38 Vic., Chap. 51, "An Act to authorize the incorporation of Boards of Trade in the Dominion," assented to 26th May, 1874 ; and the Act 39; Vic., Chap. 34, "An Act to amend the Act 37 Vic., Chap. 51, intituled 'An Act to authorize the incorporation of Boards of Trade in the Dominion,'" and assented to 12th April, 1876.

37-38 VICTORIA.

CHAPTER 51.

AN ACT TO AUTHORIZE THE INCORPORATION OF BOARDS OF TRADE IN THE DOMINION.

[Assented to 26th May, 1874.]

HER Majesty, by and with the advice and consent of the Senate and House of Commons of Canada, enacts as follows :

CHAPTER 34, 39 VICTORIA.

An Act to amend the Act thirty-seventh Victoria, chapter fifty-one, intituled : "An Act to authorize the incorporation of Boards of Trade in the Dominion."

[Assented to 12th April, 1876.]

WHEREAS it is expedient to make further provi- Preamble.
sions for the management and incorporation of Boards of Trade in the Dominion of Canada, and to provide for the incorporation and management of Chambers of Commerce in the said Dominion : Therefore Her Majesty, by and with the advice and consent of the Senate and House of Commons of Canada, enacts as follows :

"1.   Any number of persons not less than thirty, being New Section
merchants, traders, brokers, mechanics, manufacturers, in place of Section 1.
managers of banks or insurance agents, being residents Formation of
of any village, town, city, county, or of any district Boards of Trade.
(which word "district" is hereby defined to be a district established for judicial purposes by the Legislature of the Province wherein the same is situate) having a population of not less than two thousand five hundred, may associate themselves together as a Board of Trade, and appoint a Secretary, with all the privileges and powers conferred by, and subject to all the restrictions of this Act."

"2.   The persons associating themselves together as a In place of
Board of Trade under this Act shall, under their hands Section 2.
and seals, make a certificate specifying the name Certificate of formation.
assumed by the association, and by which it shall be known, the name as hereinbefore defined, of the village, town, city, county or district in which the same is situate and its business transacted, and the name of the person by them elected Secretary to the said Board of Trade."

"3. Such certificate shall be acknowledged before a notary public, commissioner appointed for receiving affidavits, or justice of the peace, by the Secretary of the said Board of Trade, and shall be forwarded to the Secretary of State, who shall cause the same to be recorded in a register to be kept for that purpose ; and a copy thereof duly certified by the Secretary of State, shall be evidence of the existence of such association."

"4. The persons named as corporators in the said certificate, and such other persons as may afterwards join them, are hereby authorized to carry into effect the objects for which such association was constituted, and to exercise the powers and privileges conferred by this Act ; and they and their associates, successors and assigns, by the name and style specified in the said certificate, shall be deemed a body corporate, with power to sue and be sued, plead and be impleaded, defend and be defended, contract and be contracted with, to make and use a common seal, and change and alter the same at pleasure, to purchase, hold, sell and convey any real or personal estate necessary for the objects of such association ; and the usual place of meeting of said corporation shall be held to be the legal domicile thereof, where service of any notice or process may be made."

"5. The officers of such Boards of Trade shall be a President, Vice-President, and Secretary, who, together with not less than eight other members, shall constitute a Council, to be called "The Council of the Board of Trade of   " (adding the name, as hereinbefore defined, of the village, town, city, county or district,) who shall have the powers and perform the duties hereinafter mentioned ; and when the foregoing provisions have been complied with, it shall be competent for a majority of the persons named as corporators in the said certificate, to hold a meeting for the election of a President, Vice-President, and members of the said Council, and to make and enact such by-laws, rules and regulations as are mentioned in the eleventh section of this Act, without the notice required in the proviso to the said section."

"6. The members of the said corporation shall hold general quarterly meetings in each year, at some place within its jurisdiction—of which notice, naming the time and place, shall be given by the Secretary of the Council for the time being, at least three days previous to such

Margin notes:

In place of Section 3. Certificate duly acknowledged to be sent to Secretary of State.

Persons incorporated to have certain powers.

Domicile.

Officers and Council of Board of Trade.

First meeting for election of officers, etc.

meeting, through one newspaper, or otherwise, as may be thought necessary by the said Council ; and at the first quarterly meeting to be held in each year, the members of the said corporation present, or a majority of them, shall then and there elect in such way as shall be fixed by the by-laws of the corporation from among the members of the corporation, one President, one Vice-President, and the Secretary, and not lest than eight other members of the Council, who, with the President, Vice-President, and Secretary, shall form the Council of the said corporation, and shall hold their offices until others shall be elected in their stead, at the next first quarterly meeting of the ensuing year, as aforesaid, or until they shall be removed from office, or shall vacate the same under the provisions of any by-laws of the corporation : Provided always, that if the said election shall not take place at such first quarterly meeting as aforesaid, the said corporation shall not be thereby dissolved, but such election may be had at any general meeting of the said corporation, to be called in the manner hereinafter provided, and the members of the Council in office shall remain members until the election shall be had."

Election of President and members of Council.

Proviso in case of failure of election.

"7.   The President and Vice-President shall, before entering upon the duties of their office, take and subscribe the following oath before the mayor of any such town or city as aforesaid, or before any Justice of the Peace :—

President & Vice-President to take oath of office

"I swear that I will faithfully and truly perform my
"duty as   of the Board of Trade, and that I
"will in all matters connected with the discharge of such
"duty, do all things, and such things only, as I shall truly
"and conscientiously believe to be adapted to promote
"the objects for which the said Board was constituted,
"according to the true intent and meaning of the same.
"So help me God."

Oath of Office.

"8.   If any member of the said Council shall die or resign his office, or be absent for six months continuously from the meetings of the said Council, it shall be lawful for the said Council at any meeting thereof to elect a member of the said corporation to be a member of the said Council, in the place of the member so dying or resigning, or being absent ; and such new member shall be so elected by a majority of the members of the said Council present at any meeting of the same, in case there is a quorum present at such meeting ; and the member

Vacation of office and filling vacancies in Council.

so elected shall hold office until the next annual election and no longer, unless re-elected."

Majority present at meetings of corporation to have full power.
"9. At any annual or general meeting of the said corporation, whether for the purpose of electing members of the Council, or for any other purpose, a majority of members present at such meeting shall be competent to do and perform all acts which, either by this Act or by any by-law of the said corporation, are or shall be directed to be done at any such general meeting."

Retirement of members.
"10. Any member of the said corporation intending to retire therefrom or resign his membership may, at any time, do so upon giving to the Secretary in writing, ten days' notice of such intention, and discharging any lawful liability which may be standing upon the books of the said corporation against him at the time of such notice."

Making by-laws and regulations; for what purpose.
"11. It shall be lawful for the said corporation, or the majority of them present at any general meeting, to make and enact such by-laws and regulations, and from time to time repeal, alter and amend the same, for the government of the said corporation, providing for the admission, subscriptions, imposing of penalties and expulsion or the retirement of members, and for the management of its Council, officers and affairs, and for the guidance of the Board of Arbitrators hereinafter mentioned, and fixing the date and place of the regular meetings of the said Council, and all other by-laws in accordance with the requirements of this Act or the laws of Canada as such majority shall deem advisable ; and such by-laws shall be binding on all members of the said corporation, its officers and servants, and on all other **Proviso: Notice of proposed by-laws to be given.** persons whomsoever lawfully under its control : Provided that no by-laws shall be made or enacted by the said corporation without notice in writing thereof having been given by one member and seconded by another member at a previous meeting, and duly entered in the books of the said corporation as a minute of the said corporation."

Who may become members of the corporation, and how.
"12. Each and every person then resident within the jurisdiction, and being or having been a merchant, broker, trader, mechanic, manufacturer, manager of a bank or insurance agent, shall be eligible to become a member of the said corporation ; and at any general meeting of the said corporation it shall be lawful for any member of the said Council or of the said corporation to propose any such person as aforesaid as a candidate for becoming a

member of the said corporation, and if such proposition
shall be carried by a majority of two-thirds of the members of the said corporation then present, he shall
thenceforth be a member of the said corporation, and
shall have all the rights and be subject to all the obli-
gations which the other members possess or are subject
to : Provided always, that any person not being a Provisoi as
merchant or trader, broker, mechanic, manufacturer, to persons
manager of a bank or insurance agent, shall be eligible not being
to become a member of the said corporation in manner traders, etc.
aforesaid, in case such person shall be recommended by
the Council of the Board of Trade at any such meeting."

"13. It shall be lawful for the said Council, or a Special gen-
majority of them, by a notice inserted in one or more ings of cor-
newspapers published within the jurisdiction, one day poration.
previous to the said meeting, or by a circular letter signed
by the Secretary of the said corporation, to each member,
and mailed one day previous to the said meeting, to call
a general meeting of the said corporation for any of the
purposes of this Act."

"14. It shall be competent to the said Council to hold Meetings of
meetings from time to time, and to adjourn the same convened,
when necessary, and at the said meetings to transact such etc
business as may, by this Act or by the by-laws of the
corporation, be assigned to them ; and such meetings of
the Council shall be convened by the Secretary, at the
instance of the President, or upon the request of any two
members of the Council : and the said Council shall, in Powers.
addition to the powers hereby expressly conferred on
them, have such powers as shall be assigned to them by
any by-law of the corporation, except only the power of Exception.
enacting or altering any by-law, or admitting any member, which shall be done in the manner provided for by
this Act, and no other : and any five or more members
of the Council, lawfully met, shall be a quorum, and any Quorum.
majority of such quorum may do all things within the
powers of the Council : and at all meetings of the said
Council, and at all general meetings of the corporation,
the President, or in his absence, the Vice-President, or if Who to pre-
both be absent, any member of the Council then present side.
who may be chosen for the occasion shall preside, and in
all cases of equality of votes upon any division, have a Casting vote
casting vote."

"15. It shall be the duty of the Council to frame such Council to
by-laws, rules, and regulations as shall seem to the said frame by-

16

Council best adapted to promote the welfare of the said corporation, and the purposes of this Act, and to submit the same for adoption at a general meeting of the said corporation called for that purpose, in the manner hereinbefore provided."

Recovery of subscriptions, etc.

"16. All subscriptions of members due to the said corporation, under any by-law, all penalties incurred under any by-law, by any person bound thereby, and all other sums of money due to the said corporation, shall be paid to the Secretary thereof, and in default of payment, may be recovered in any action brought in the name of the said corporation; and it shall only be necessary in such action to allege that such person is indebted to the said corporation in the sum of money, the amount of such arrearage on account of such subscription, penalty or otherwise, whereby an action hath accrued to the said corporation by virtue of this Act."

Proof in action brought in such case.

"17. On the trial or hearing of any such action, it shall be sufficient for the said corporation to prove that the defendant at the time of making such demand was or had been a member of the said corporation, and that the amount claimed by such subscription, penalty or otherwise was standing unpaid upon the books of the said corporation."

Meetings of Council to be open to corporation.

Record thereof.

"18. The meetings of the members of the Council shall be open to all members of the said corporation who may attend at the same, but who shall take no part in any proceedings thereat ; and minutes of the proceedings at all meetings, whether of the said Council or the said corporation, shall be entered in books to be kept for that purpose by the Secretary of the said corporation ; and the entry thereof shall be signed by the President of the said Council or such other person who at the time shall preside over any such meeting, and such books shall be open at all reasonable hours to any member of the said corporation, free from any charge."

Board of Arbitration.

Powers.

"19. At the same time and times as are hereby appointed for the election of the said Council, and in the same manner, it shall be lawful for the members of the said corporation to elect from their number twelve persons, who shall form a board, which shall be called "The Board of Arbitration," and any three of whom shall have power to arbitrate upon, and make their award in any commercial case or difference which shall be voluntarily referred to them by the parties concerned ; and whenever any such parties shall agree to bind themselves, by bond or otherwise, to submit the matter in dispute between them to the decision of the said Board of Arbitrators, such submission shall be understood to be made to any three members of the said board, who may, either by the special order of the said board, or by virtue of any general rules adopted by them, or under any by-law of the said corporation touching the consideration of any cases so submitted, be appointed to hear, arbitrate and decide upon the case or cases so submitted to them ; and such decision shall be binding upon the said board and the parties making the submission ; and any such submission shall be according to the form set forth in the schedule to this Act, or in words to the same effect." Form of sub mission to Board.

"20. The several members of the said Board of Arbitration shall, before they act as such, take and subscribe before the President or Vice-President of the said corporation, an oath that they will faithfully, impartially and diligently, perform their duties as members of the said Board of Arbitration, and such oath shall be kept among the documents of the said corporation." Members of Board to be sworn.

"21. Any member of the Council of the said corporation may, at the same time, be a member of the said Board of Arbitration." Members of Council may be arbitrators.

"22. The three members appointed to hear any case submitted for arbitration, as aforesaid, or any two of them, shall have full power to examine upon oath (which oath any one of such three members is hereby empowered to administer) any party or witness who, appearing before them shall be so examined, and shall give their award thereupon in writing ; and their decision, or that of any two of them, given in such award shall bind the parties according to the terms of submission and the provisions of this Act." Powers of arbitrators as to examination in hearing cases.
Award.

"23. It shall be lawful for the Council of the said corporation to appoint five persons to constitute a Board of Examiners to examine applicants for the office of Inspector of flour and meal, or of any other article subject to inspection, and for the said Council to do all such other acts, matters and things connected with the Inspection of flour and meal or any other article, and have as Power of Council to appoint.

full power and be subject to the same conditions as those conferred upon and required of the Councils of the Boards of Trade by virtue of the Act thirty-sixth Victoria, Chapter forty-nine, intituled "An Act to amend and consolidate, and to extend to the whole Dominion of Canada, the Laws respecting the Inspection of certain "staple articles of Canadian produce ;" and the said Examiners and Inspector shall also be subject to all the conditions, requirements, oaths, matters and things (touching their office) set forth in the said Act."

36 V., c. 49. But see now 37 V., c. 45 substituted for it.

Oaths and affirmations. "24. Any person who may, by law in other cases, make a solemn affirmation, may make such solemn affirmation in any case where by this Act an oath is required ; and any person hereby authorized to administer an oath may, in such case as aforesaid, administer such solemn affirmation ; and any person who shall wilfully swear or affirm falsely in any case where an oath or solemn affirmation is required or authorized by this Act shall be guilty of wilful perjury."

Boards of Trade registered under this Act may affiliate with Dominion Board of Trade. "25. It shall be competent for any Board of Trade duly registered as aforesaid under the provisions of this Act, to become affiliated with the Dominion Board of Trade, on duly complying with all the terms and requirements of that organization, and to be represented at all its ordinary or special general meetings, which may be

Proviso. held from time to time : Provided always that the delegates or representatives to the said Dominion Board of Trade shall be elected at a general meeting duly convened, of the said Board desiring such affiliation as aforesaid."

Her Majesty's rights saved. "26. Nothing in this Act shall affect the rights of Her Majesty, Her Heirs or Successors, or of any party or person whomsoever, such rights only accepted as are herein expressly mentioned and affected."

Act to apply to Chambers of Commerce "27. Each, all and every of the provisions of this Act shall apply to the incorporation and management of the commercial institutions styled 'Chambers of Commerce' now existing or which hereafter may be called into existence in the Dominion of Canada, as fully and effectually as if the words 'Chamber of Commerce' or 'Chambers of Commerce' appeared therein in lieu and place of the words 'Board of Trade' or 'Boards of Trade,' wheresoever the same appear respectively."

SCHEDULE.

FORM OF A SUBMISSION TO THE BOARD OF ARBITRATION.

Know all men that the undersigned   and the undersigned (if there be more parties, that is, more separate interests, mention them) having a difference as to the respective rights of the said parties, as in the case hereunto subjoined, have agreed and bound themselves under a penalty of   dollars to perform the award to be made by the Board of Arbitration of the Board of Trade of   in the case aforesaid, under the penalty aforesaid to be paid by the party refusing to perform such award, to the party ready and willing to perform the same.

In witness whereof the said parties have hereunto set their hands and affixed their seals at the   of   on the   day of   , A. D. 18 .

A. B.   [L.S.]
C. D.   [L.S.]
E. F.   [L.S.]

FORM OF OATH TO BE TAKEN BY MEMBERS OF THE BOARD OF ARBITRATION.

I swear that I will faithfully, impartially and diligently perform my duty as a member of the Board of Arbitration of the Board of Trade of   , and that ⸳ will, in all cases in which I shall act as arbitrator, give a true and just award, according to the best of my judgment and ability, without fear, favor or affection, of or for any party or person whomsoever. So help me God.

BY-LAWS.

I. The Annual General Meeting of Members of the "New Westminster Board of Trade" shall be held on the 22nd February at 7:30 P. M. The regular Quarterly Meetings of the Board shall be held on the 22nd February, 22nd May, 22nd August, and 22nd November in each year, and at the time prescribed for the Annual General Meeting. Should the day of Meeting, either Annual or Quarterly, fall on Sunday or a legal holiday the Meeting shall be held the following day.

QUORUM.

II. At any General Meeting Seven Members present in person shall constitute a quorum for the transaction of business. At Council Meetings Five shall form a quorum (including the President, Vice-President or Member elected to act as Chairman). Should a quorum not be formed by 8 P. M. on any occasion the Meeting shall stand adjourned for one day.

PLACE OF MEETING.

III. The place of Meeting shall be arranged from time to time by the Council, and mentioned in the Notices calling each Meeting, until such time as a regular place of Meeting shall have been determined by the Council.

ORDER OF BUSINESS.

IV. Reading Minutes of last Meeting.

Reports and Communications.

Elections to fill Vacancies.

Nomination and election of new Members.

Unfinished business.

Miscellaneous business.

AUDIT.

V. At the regular Quarterly Meeting held in November of each year the President shall appoint a Committee of three to audit the books and accounts of the Secretary-Treasurer for presentation at the Annual General Meeting.

MOTIONS.

VI. All Motions, except those for previous question, post-ponement or adjournment, shall be made in writing; and no debate shall be permitted, except on a motion regularly moved and seconded; every motion made in writing shall be read by the proposer in his place previous to offering it to the President.

(a). No Member shall speak twice on the same subject except by permission or by way of explanation.

(b). A Member may call for the division on any motion, should any doubt exist as to the ruling of the President.

ALTERATION OF BY-LAWS.

VII. Notice to amend any By-Law or to introduce a new one shall be made in writing at the regular Quarterly Meeting next previous to the one at which it is intended to be considered. Any such notice as aforesaid must contain in full "the wording of the proposed amendment or addition."

SUBSCRIPTIONS.

VIII. (a). The Annual Subscription of Members shall be twelve dollars, payable by quarterly instalments of $3.00 in advance, to the Secretary at the office of the Council of the Board of Trade.

(b). Members in arrears for three months shall be deemed delinquent and their names shall be posted up in the office of the "Board of Trade" for one month, and the Secretary shall notify them to that effect. After thirty days from the date of such notice and posting, their names shall be liable to be removed from the "List of Members."

(c). A list of delinquent Members (if any) shall be read at each Quarterly Meeting, and their names duly entered on the minutes of said Meeting.

ARBITRATIONS.

IX. (1). Before any arbitration can be entered upon the parties shall execute a bond of submission as provided by Statute here-inbefore expressed.

(2). In case of arbitration the Arbitrators shall be selected from the "Board of Arbitration" as follows: Each party shall choose one arbitrator and the third arbitrator shall be drawn by lot, from the remainder of said Board, by the Secretary of the Board, in the presence of the parties, unless a third shall have been agreed upon or chosen by the Arbitrators within three days after the submission of the parties.

(3). The three Arbitrators shall sit together unless the parties shall consent to the matter being heard by one or two Arbitrators alone.

(4). The decision of the majority of the Arbitrators, when more than two sit, shall be final, and binding on both parties.

(5). The fees for Arbitration shall be as follows :—

(a). For every meeting where the cause is not proceeded with, but an enlargement or postponement is made at the request of either party, not less than.......$ 2 00

Nor more than............................ 4 00

(b). For every day's sitting, to consist of not less than six hours, not less than......................$ 5 00

Nor more than............................ 10 00

(c). For every sitting not extending to six hours (fractional parts of hours being excluded) where the arbitration is actually proceeded with, for each—for each hour occupied in such proceedings, at the rate of not less than......................................$ 1 00

Nor more than............................ 1 50

Vide British Columbia Statutes 1879, Chap. X., pp. 31.

(6). If any Arbitrator who has been duly selected (in manner aforesaid) to act, refuses or neglects to attend such arbitration, he shall be liable to pay to the Secretary of said Board a fine of $5 for each and every day on which he neglects to attend such arbitration unless relieved by the Council. All fines inflicted as aforesaid to form part of the revenue of the Board of Trade.

PROXIES.

X. (1). At all meetings of the Board no member shall be entitled to vote who has not paid all dues belonging to him.

(2). Members in good standing shall be entitled to hold two proxies, and no more, for the purpose of voting at any meeting.

(3). All proxies must be in writing and shall be deposited with the Secretary on or before the day of the meeting, and may be either Special or General.

EXPULSION OF MEMBERS.

XI. (1). Any member who is declared an insolvent shall thereby be considered as retiring from the Board but shall be entitled to be nominated for re-election at any time.

(2). Any member can be expelled by the vote of three-fourths (¾ths) of the members present at any meeting specially called for the purpose, at which not less than one-half (½) of the whole number of members are present either in person or represented by their proxies.

ENTRANCE FEES.

XII. On and after the first day of September of the current year, any person desirous of joining the Board of Trade shall pay an entrance fee of ten dollars ($10.00) in addition to his annual subscription.

CUSTOMS OF THE PORT.

RATES OF COMMISSION.

XIII. Whenever no special agreement exists, the following shall be collectable :—

1. On purchase of stocks, bonds, and all kinds of securities, including the drawing of bills for payment of the same.....................................2½ per cent.

2. On sale of stocks, bonds, and all kinds of securities, including remittances on bills and guarantee..2½ per cent.

3. On purchase and sale of specie, gold-dust, and bullion.......................................1 per cent.

4. On sale of bills of exchange, with endorsement....................................3½ per cent.

5. On sale of bills of exchange, without endorsement......................................1 per cent.

6. For endorsing bills of exchange, when desired..2½ per cent.

7. On sale of produce, &c., from California, Oregon, Washington Territory, Sandwich Island ports, and other Pacific Coast ports, with guarantee......7½ per cent.

8. On sale of merchandise from other ports, with guarantee....................................10 per cent.

9. On goods received on consignment, and afterwards withdrawn........................ ....3½ per cent.

10. On purchase and shipment of merchandise, with funds on hand, on cost and charges.................5 per cent.

11. On purchase, and shipment of merchandise without funds, on cost and charges..................7½ per cent.

12. For collecting and remitting delayed or litigated accounts..................................10 per cent.

13. For collecting freight by vessels from foreign ports, on amount collected...........................5 per cent.

14. For collecting general claims ....5 per cent

15. For collecting general average—on the first $20,000 or any smaller amount ....5 per cent.

16. For collecting general average—on any excess over $20,000.....................................2½ per cent.

17. On purchase or sale of vessels.................5 per cent.

18. For "Port Agency" to vessels with cargo or passengers from foreign ports, as under :
    On vessels under 200 tons register ....$ 50.00
    On do of 200 to 300 tons do........ ..... 100.00
    On do of 300 to 500 tons do............. 150.00
    On do over 500 tons ;.................. 200.00

19. For disbursements of vessels by consignees with funds on hand................................2½ per cent.

20. For disbursements of vessels by consignees without funds on hand..............................5 per cent.

21. For procuring freight or passengers............5 per cent.

22. For chartering vessels, on amount of freight, actual or estimated, to be considered as due when the "Charter Parties" or memorandum of their conditions, &c., are signed......................................5 per cent.

23. On giving Bonds for vessels under attachment in litigated cases, on amount of the liability...........2½ per cent.

24. For landing and reshipping goods from vessels in distress, on invoice value, or in its absence, on market value ....5 per cent.

25. For receiving and forwarding goods,—on invoice amount................................2½ per cent.

26. For advancing on freight to be earned.........5 per cent.

27. For effecting marine insurance,—on the amount insured.......................................½ per cent.

28. The foregoing Commissions to be exclusive of Brokerage, and every charge actually incurred.

29. Vessels to pay clerk hire and the labor on wharf, sorting and delivering cargo.

30. The receipt of Bills of Lading to be considered equivalent to receipt of the goods.

RATES OF STORAGE ON MERCHANDISE.

STORAGE PER MONTH.

XIV. On measurement goods 50 cents per ton of forty cubic feet (40 c. ft.) On heavy goods 50 cents per ton of 2,240 lbs. Or in either case the amount actually paid if more. The consignee to have the option of charging by measurement or weight.

Any fraction of a month to be charged as a month.

REGULATIONS.

XV. (a.) Concerning the delivery of merchandise, payment of freight, &c.: When no express stipulation exists per bill of lading, goods are to be considered as deliverable on shore.

(b.) Freight on all goods to be paid, or secured to the satisfaction of the captain or consignee of the vessel prior to the delivery of the goods.

(c.) After delivery to the purchaser of goods sold no claims for damage, deficiency, or other cause, shall be admissable after goods sold and delivered have once left the city.

. (d.) When foreign bills of lading expressly stipulate that the freight shall be paid in a specific coin, then the same must be procured if required, or its equivalent given,—the rate to be determined by the current value at the time at the banks.

---

37 VICTORIA, CHAPTER 32.

An Act to provide for the appointment of Port Wardens at certain Ports of the Dominion.

[Assented to Tuesday, 26th May, 1874.]

WHEREAS, the increasing trade and business in many of the Ports of the Dominion, at which no provision now exists for the appointment of Port Wardens, renders it necessary to make such provision: Therefore Her Majesty, by and with the advice and consent of the Senate and House of Commons of Canada, enacts as follows :— *Preamble*

1. The Governor in Council may, from time to time, determine at what ports in the Dominion, it is expedient that Port Wardens should be appointed, and at and for any such port a Port Warden may be appointed under this Act, by the Governor: Provided always that this Act shall not apply to the Ports of Quebec, Montreal and St. John, New Brunswick, for which provision is already made. *Governor may appoint Port Wardens. Certain ports excepted.*

2. The Port Warden shall receive no fees whatever, other than such as strictly appertain to the business of his office; all such fees shall be recorded in his books, and he shall make a certified annual return to the Minister of Marine and Fisheries, of the receipts and expenses of his office, and a report of the doings of his office, within seven days after thirty-first day of December in each year. *Fees to Port Warden. His annual return to Minister.*

3. The Port Warden shall, at his own expense, keep an office during the season of navigation, and shall have a seal of office and the necessary books, in which all his acts as Port Warden shall be recorded, which books shall be open for inspection on payment of a fee of twenty-five cents. *His office books and seal.*

4. It shall be the duty of the Port Warden, on being notified and requested by any of the parties interested, to proceed in person on board of any vessel for the pur- *Port Warden on request to examine*

pose of examining the condition and stowage of her cargo ; and if there be any goods damaged on board such vessel, he shall inquire, examine and ascertain the cause or causes of such damage, and make a memorandum thereof, and enter the same in full on the books of his office.

5. The master of any vessel which has broken bulk for the purpose of lightening or other necessary purpose, previous to her arrival in any harbour for which there is then a Port Warden, shall, immediately on the discovery of any damaged cargo, proceed to have a survey held on the same in the manner herein prescribed, before the same shall be moved out of the place in which it was originally stowed ; and if, after the arrival in port of any vessel from beyond the seas, or from a passage over any of the great lakes contiguous to the Province of Ontario, which has not had occasion to lighten, break bulk, or otherwise discharge any portion of her cargo before coming into the harbour, the hatches of such vessel shall have been first opened by any person not a Port Warden, and the cargo or any part thereof shall come from on board such ship in a damaged condition, these facts shall be prima facie evidence that such damage occurred in consequence of improper stowage or negligence on the part of the persons in charge of the vessel ; and such default shall, until the contrary be shewn, be chargeable to the owner, master or other person interested as part owner or master of the said vessel.

6. The Port Warden shall, when required, proceed to any ship, steamer or other vessel, warehouse, dwelling or wharf, and examine any merchandise, vessel, material, produce or other property, said to have been damaged on board any vessel, and enquire, examine and ascertain the cause of such damage, make a memorandum thereof, and of such property, and record in the books of his office a full and correct statement thereof.

7. The Port Warden shall, when required, be surveyor on any vessel which may have suffered wreck or damage, or which shall be deemed unfit to proceed on her voyage ; he shall examine the hull, spars, rigging and all appurtenances thereof, shall specify what damage has occurred, and record in the books of his office a full and particular account of all surveys held on such vessel ; he shall call to his assistance, if necessary, in such survey, one or more carpenters, sail-makers, riggers, shipwrights or

(marginal notes:)
and note the condition of cargo, &c. on any vessel.

Survey if bulk has been broken before arrival in Port.

What shall be prima facie evidence of improper stowage.

Port Warden on request to ascertain cause of damage to any goods.

To be a surveyor of wrecks or damaged vessels

other persons skilled in their profession, who shall each be entitled to a fee not exceeding five dollars, to aid him in the examination and survey; but no such surveyor shall be interested in the case. The Port Warden shall also, if required, be surveyor of the repairs necessary to render such vessel seaworthy, and his certificate that these repairs have been properly made shall be evidence that the vessel is seaworthy. *To see that vessel are seaworthy.*

8. The Port Warden shall have cognizance of all matters relating to the surveys of vessels and their cargoes, arriving in port damaged, and when requested shall, on payment of the regular fee, give certificates of such surveys. *Surveys of damaged vessels and cargoes.*

9. The master of any vessel intending to load grain in bulk, for any port not within the limits of inland navigation, nor within the Dominion of Canada, shall, before taking in any such grain, notify the Port Warden from time to time, while the different chambers are being prepared, to survey and inspect the said vessel as well as the dunnage and lining boards ; the Port Warden in such case shall ascertain whether such vessel is in a fit state to receive and carry the cargo intended for her to its destination ; he shall record in his books the condition of the vessel ; if he finds that she is not fit to carry the cargo in safety, he shall state what repairs are necessary to render her seaworthy; before beginning to load each chamber he shall be careful to see that it is properly dunnaged and lined, and provided with shifting boards, and that the board and plank used for these purposes have been properly seasoned ; he shall examine the pumps and see that they are properly lined and dunnaged ; he shall enter in the books of his office all particulars connected with these surveys, and grant the necessary certificates. *Duty of master of vessel loading with grain in bulk for port out of Canada; and duty of Port Warden*

10. It shall be the duty of the Port Warden, when required, to decide what amount of dunnage is necessary below cargo, and also between wheat and other grain, and the flour to be stowed over it, and his certificate that such dunnage has been used, shall be prima facie evidence of the good stowage of the cargo so far as these points are concerned. *Duty of Port Warden as to dunnage.*

11. The master of any vessel, wholly or partly laden with grain, for any port not within the limits of inland navigation, nor within the Dominion of Canada, shall, *Further duties of master and*

Port Warden as to grain vessels. before proceeding on his voyage, or clearing at the Custom House for the same, notify the Port Warden, whose duty it shall then be to proceed on board such vessel, and examine whether she is in a fit state to proceed to sea or not ; if she is found unfit, the Port Warden shall state in what particulars, and on what conditions only she will be deemed in a fit state to leave, and shall notify the master not to leave the port until the required conditions have been fulfilled ; and in case of the master refusing or neglecting to fulfil the same, the Port Warden shall notify the Collector of Customs, in order that no clearance may be granted for the vessel until such required conditions have been fulfilled, and a certificate thereof granted by the Port Warden or his deputy.

Valuing and measuring vessels by Port Warden 12. The Port Warden shall, when required, estimate the value and measurement of any vessel, when the same is in dispute or otherwise needed, and shall record the same in the books of his office.

Duty of auctioneer selling condemned vessels, mater. ials or goods. 13. It shall be the duty of every auctioneer making a sale of any vessel condemned, or ship's materials, or goods damaged on board a ship or vessel, whether sea-going or of inland navigation, sold for benefit of underwriters or others concerned, in any harbour for which there is then a Port Warden, to file a statement of the same at the office of the Port Warden within ten days after such sale ; no underwriters' sale shall take place until after at least two days' public advertisement or notice, and such sale shall not be at an hour earlier than eleven, nor later than three o'clock in the day.

Port Warden to arbitrate between master and consignee, &c. 14. It shall be the duty of the Port Warden, when required in writing by all parties in interest, to hear and arbitrate upon any difficulty or matter in dispute between the master or consignee of any vessel, and any proprietor, shipper or consignee of the cargo, and to keep a record thereof.

Sale of damaged vessels or goods on account of underwriters. 15. No goods, vessels or other property at a place where there is a Port Warden, shall be sold as damaged for account of underwriters, unless a regular survey and condemnation has previously been had, and the Port Warden shall in all such cases be one of the surveyors.

Notice by Port Warden 16. Before proceeding to act in any case in the performance of his duties, the Port Warden shall give reasonable notice, where practicable, to all parties interested or concerned in the case.

17. All notices, requests, or requirements to, or from the Port Warden, must be given in writing, and a reasonable time before action is required. *And to him.*

18. The Port Warden may, in any case where he thinks it right and necessary, initiate proceedings, and hold surveys, and obtain process, as if required by the parties concerned under the provisions of this Act,—and whenever the Port Warden is mentioned in any provision of this Act, such provision shall always be understood to apply to any Deputy Port Warden, if there is such. *Port Warden may initiate proceedings. Deputy Port Warden.*

19. On the demand of any party interested, the Port Warden shall furnish certificates in writing, under his hand, of any matters of record in his office ; he shall also furnish, when required, copies of any entries in his books or documents filed in his office, upon payment of a reasonable compensation. *Port Warden to furnish copies of documents, &c., in his office.*

20. On application, the Port Warden shall supply, to any master of a vessel arriving in the harbour, a copy of the regulations relating to the office of Port Warden once in each year. *And copies of regulations of harbour.*

21. In all matters regarding surveys, and other matters concerning the value, state, or classification of vessels and like subjects, the Port Warden shall conform to, and be governed by, the regulations of Lloyd's, so far as they are applicable to the circumstances of the case. *To conform to regulations of Lloyd's.*

22. Should any dispute arise between the Port Warden and any party interested in any case where his presence has been required, either party may appeal to the council of the board of trade or chamber of commerce, where there is one, and it shall be the duty of the Secretary of such board or chamber, on a requisition being presented to him to that effect, to summon forthwith a meeting of the said council who, or not less than three of them, shall immediately investigate and report on the case submitted to them, and their determination or that of a majority of them, made in writing, shall be final and conclusive. *Disputes with Port Warden to be settled by board of trade.*

23. The party against whom the council of the board of trade or chamber of commerce shall decide shall pay all the expenses, and the council shall determine the amount of fees or charges payable in each case, which shall never exceed twenty dollars. *Costs in such case.*

156444

Certificates of Port Warden to be evidence.

24. All certificates issued under the hand of the Port Warden or his deputy, and sealed with the seal of his office, referring to matters recorded in his books, shall be received as prima facie evidence of the existence and contents of such record, in any court in Canada.

Tariff of fees to be paid to Port Warden to be made by board of trade or Governor in Council.

25. The council of the board of trade or chamber of commerce, if there is one, may, from time to time, establish a tariff of fees to be paid to the Port Warden for services performed by him and his deputies, by the masters or owners of sea-going vessels, and by others in respect of whom the duties of the said Port Warden are required to be performed,—which tariff, being first approved by the Governor in Council, shall be enforced until repealed or altered by the said Governor in Council, or by the said council of the board of trade or chamber of commerce, as it may be at any time, with the approval of the Governor in Council ; and when there is no board of trade or chamber of commerce, the Governor in Council shall make such tariff ; but such fees shall not exceed the rates hereinafter mentioned, that is to say:—

Maximum rates.

1. For every survey and the certificate thereof by the Port Warden and his assistant, of the hatches and cargo of any vessel, or of the hull, spars and rigging thereof, or the survey of damaged goods, a fee, including the

Survey of vessel, damaged goods, etc.

certificate thereof, not exceeding eight dollars each, and such further sum, not exceeding five dollars, as may be payable to shipwrights or other skilled persons employed by him :

Valuation and inspection of vessel.

2. For every valuation of a vessel for average, and every inspection of a vessel intended to load, a fee to be graduated according to the tonnage of such vessel, but not in any case to exceed ten dollars :

Hearing and settling disputes.

3. For hearing and settling disputes of which the Port Warden is authorized to take cognizance, and for the fees on appeal to the council of the board of trade or chamber of commerce, a sum to be graduated according to the value of the thing or the amount in dispute, but in no case to exceed twenty dollars :

Rates may be altered, etc., by board of trade or Governor in Council.

4. The foregoing maximum rates, comprehending the fees for the incidental proceeding, certificates and copies, may be altered and apportioned, and the particular service distinguished, and the fee therefor assigned, and the person by whom the same shall be paid, may be indicated in such a way as the council of the board of trade or

chamber of commerce may from time to time appoint ;
and all rates and fees so established shall be subject to
the approval of the Governor in Council, who shall have
power from time to time to disallow or mcdify and alter
such fees and rates.

26. The penalty for any and every infraction or **Penalties for contravention of ss. 9, 11 and 13. Recovery and appropriation of.**
breach of the ninth or of the eleventh section of this Act,
shall be the sum of eight hundred dollars ; and for every
infraction or breach of the thirteenth section of this Act,
the sum of twenty dollars ; and any and every such penalty as aforesaid shall be recoverable in the manner prescribed by the Interpretation Act, in cases where penalties are imposed, and the recovery is not otherwise
provided for ; and the whole of any pecuniary penalty
imposed by this Act shall belong to the Crown, and shall
be paid over to the Receiver General, by the officer or
person receiving it, and shall be appropriated in such
manner as the Governer in Council may direct.

27. The Port Warden shall have such other and fur- **Further duties of Port Warden under regulations of Governor in Council.**
ther duties as may be assigned to him from time to time
by any regulations made by order of the Governor in
Council ; and the council of the board of trade or chamber
of commerce may, from time to time, make such sugges-
tions to the Governor as they may deem expedient, with
respect to and such other and further duties, or any
modification of the duties hereinbefore assigned to the
Port Warden for the harbour ; and such other and further
duties may be assigned or such modification made, by
Order in Council accordingly: any such Order in Council
may be amended or repealed, and new provision made,
and any regulations so made shall, while unrepealed,
have the force of law, as if contained in this Act.

28. No officer of Customs shall grant a clearance to **Clearance not to be granted to any vessel carrying grain unless the requirements of this Act have been complied with.**
any vessel wholly or partly loaded with grain, for the
purpose of enabling her to leave the harbour for any port
not within the limits of inland navigation, nor within the
Dominion of Canada, unless nor until the master of such
vessel produces to him a certificate from the Port Warden or his deputy, to the effect that all the requirements
of this act have been fully complied with if such grain be
laden in bulk; nor unless or until such master produces
to him a certificate from the Port Warden or his deputy,
that all the requirements of this Act, have been fully
complied with, if such vessel be wholly or partly laden
with grain, otherwise than wholly or partly in bulk, and

if the vessel wholly or partly loaded with grain attempts to leave the harbour for any port not within the limits of inland navigation, nor within the Dominion of Canada, without a clearance, any officer of Customs, or any person acting under the direction of the Minister of Marine and Fisheries, or the chief officer of the River Police, may detain such vessel until such certificate is produced to him.

Interpreta- 29. The expression "the harbour" in this Act, means
tion. the harbour for which the Port Warden is appointed ; the expression "the board of trade or chamber of commerce" means the board of trade or chamber of commerce for the city or town or place adjoining the harbour for which the Port Warden is appointed.

Short title. 30. This Act may be cited as "The General Port Wardens' Act, 1874."

Whereas, by an Order in Council of the 8th March, 1875, the ports of Victoria and Esquimalt, in British Columbia, are determined as ports to which the provisions of the Act 37 Vic., chap. 32, providing for the appointment of Port Wardens shall apply; and whereas under the 25th section of the said Act the Governor-General in Council did on the 26th April, 1876, establish a tariff of fees to be paid to the Port Warden for services performed by him and his deputies by the masters and owners of sea-going vessels, and by others in respect of whom the duties of the said Port Warden are required to be performed, that is to say:—Vide Orders in Council, 40 Vic., pp. LXXVI, (76) 1877.

And whereas the "New Westminster Board of Trade" has been incorporated in manner hereinbefore described, said Board of Trade does hereby (subject to ratification of Governor-General in Council and under the authority of the 25th section aforesaid) make the following tariff of fees for said Port Warden:—

TARIFF OF FEES COLLECTIBLE.

1. First survey of hatches with certificate under seal...$ 5.00

2. Every subsequent survey of cargo with certificate under seal 2.00

3. Survey of cargo where hatches have not been previously surveyed, including certificate under seal... 5.00

4. Every survey of damaged goods on the wharf, or in store, value under $200, and certificate under seal... 3.00

5. Every survey of damaged goods on the wharf, or in store, value $200 and under $500, and certificate under seal.................................... 4.00

6. Every survey of damaged goods on the wharf, or in store, value $500 and over, and certificate under seal 5.00

7. Survey of vessel damaged or arriving in distress, including certificate under seal 10.00

8. Every subsequent survey, with certificate under seal.. 5.00

9. Valuation of a vessel for average, under 200 tons register, including certificate under seal.......... 5.00

10. Valuation of a vessel for average of 200 tons and under 500 tons, with certificate under seal........ 7.50

11. Valuation of a vessel for average of 500 tons and upwards, with certificate under seal.............. 10.00

12. Survey of cargo reported to have shifted, including certificate under seal 5.00

13. Extra copy of certificate, when required, and under seal.................................... 1.00

14. Hearing and settling disputes between master and consignee of ship and owners of cargo the Port Warden shall be entitled to demand and receive:—
    Value of cargo under $200................... 2.00
    do   do $200 to $500................. 3.00
    do   do $500 to $1000 .... 4.00
    do   do $1000 and over 5.00

15. Filing papers of auctioneers, &c., each 25

16. Ascertaining if vessel is seaworthy, including certificate under seal 10.00

17. Survey, that repairs ordered, if not seaworthy, have been made, inclusive of certificate under seal:—
    200 tons and under......................... 3.00
    Over 200 tons 5.00

18. General superintendence of a vessel loading, with certificate under seal 5.00

XVII   HARBOUR MASTER.

Vide Act 36 Vic., chap. 9, assented to 3rd May, 1873.
  do   37 Vic., chap. 34, . do   26th May, 1874.
  do   38 Vic., chap. 30,   do   8th April, 1875.

The Board of Trade having no control under this head the
Acts as amended are consolidated for the information and general guidance of members.

HARBOUR MASTERS' ACTS CONSOLIDATED.

AN ACT TO PROVIDE FOR THE APPOINTMENT OF HAR-
BOUR MASTERS FOR CERTAIN PORTS IN THE PROV-
INCES OF QUEBEC, ONTARIO, BRITISH COLUMBIA,
AND PRINCE EDWARD ISLAND.
[Assented to 26th May, 1874.]

AND

AN ACT TO AMEND THE ACTS THIRTY-SIXTH VICTORIA,
CHAPTER NINE, AND THIRTY-SEVENTH VICTORIA,
CHAPTER, THIRTY-FOUR, RESPECTING THE APPOINT-
MENT OF HARBOUR MASTERS.
[Assented to 8th April, 1875.]

Preamble   HER MAJESTY, by and with the advice and consent
of the Senate and House of Commons of Canada, enacts
as follows:—

Interpreta-   1. In the construction, and for the purposes of this
tion.   Act (if not inconsistent with the context or subject matter), the following terms shall have the respective mean-
ings hereinafter assigned to them, that is to say:—

"Ship" shall include every description of vessel used
in navigation not propelled by oars;

"Master" shall include every person (except a pilot)
having command or charge of a ship;

"Harbor Master" shall mean a Harbour Master appointed under this Act;

"Port" shall mean a port to which this Act applies.

2. The Governor may, from time to time, appoint a fit and proper person to be Harbour Master for any port in any of the Provinces of Quebec, Ontario, British Columbia or Prince Edward Island, to which this Act applies. *Governor may appoint Harbour Masters.*

3. Every Harbour Master appointed under this Act shall be under the control of the Minister of Marine and Fisheries, to whom he shall furnish a report in writing and on oath, as soon as possible after the thirty-first day of December in each year, of his doings in office, and of the fees of office received by him during such year. *Annual report of Harbour Masters to Minister of Marine, &c.*

4. The rights, powers and duties of the Harbour Master for any port shall be such as may from time to time be conferred and imposed upon him by rules and regulations made by the Governor in Council for the government of his office and of the port for which he is appointed, and for his remuneration; which rules and regulations the Governor in Council is hereby authorized and empowered to make, and from time to time to alter, amend or repeal; and any such rules and regulations may be so made to apply to any one or more ports to which this Act then applies, or may be afterwards extended by order in Council to any such port. *Regulations by Governor in Council.*

5. The Governor in Council may in and by any rule or regulation made under the next preceding section, impose any reasonable penalty, not exceeding in any case one hundred dollars, for the breach of such rule or regulation, with, in case of a continuing breach, a further penalty, not exceeding in any case ten dollars for every twelve hours during which such breach continues, but so that no such rule or regulation shall impose a minimum penalty; and every breach of any such rule or regulation shall be deemed a contravention of this Act, and every such penalty shall be held to be a penalty imposed by this Act. *Regulations may impose penalties.*

6. The Harbour Master for any such port shall furnish copies of the rules and regulations made under the next preceding section, and then in force, to every licensed pilot of the port, who shall give one of such copies to the master of every ship which he shall take in charge. *Copies to be furnished to Pilots.*

7. It shall be the duty of the Harbour Master of any such port to prosecute every person violating any rules or regulations made by the Governor in Council under this Act. *Prosecutions for infraction.*

"8. The Harbour Master for any port shall be re-munerated for his services solely by the fees hereinafter mentioned, or such portion thereof as he may, from time to time, be authorized to retain by the rules and regula-tions made by the Governor in Council under the fourth section of this Act; and for and in respect of all ships entering a port or harbour to which this Act applies, and at which a Harbour Master is appointed, and discharging or taking in cargo, ballast, stores, wood or water, there shall be paid the following fees, that is to say:—

For every ship of fifty tons register or under, fifty cents;

For every ship over fifty tons an,   er one hun-dred tons register, one dollar;

For every ship over one hundred tons and not over two hundred tons register, one dollar and fifty cents;

For every ship over two hundred tons and not over three hundred tons register, two dollars;

For every ship over three hundred tons and not over four hundred tons register, two dollars and fifty cents;

For every ship over four hundred tons and not over five hundred tons register, three dollars;

For every ship over five hundred tons an'   'c' 'er seven hundred tons, four dollars;

For every ship over seven hundred tons regis' , five dollars;

And such fees shall also be payable for ships with cargo and steamers passing through or arriving at the harbours of Sorel, St. Johns, Three Rivers or Lachine, in the Province of Quebec; and the Governor may, from time to time, appoint a fit and proper person to be Har-bour Master at each of the said harbours."

Salary, how fixed. 9. The salary or remuneration of each Ha '   ir Mas-ter, appointed under this Act, shall be, from time to time, fixed by Order of the Governor in Council, but shall not exceed six hundred dollars, and shall be subject to the provisions hereinafter made.

Balance to be paid over 10. The Harbour Master of each port shall pay over as soon as possible after the thirty-first day of December in each year to the Receiver-General, to form part of the _{tc Con. Rev. Fund.} Consolidated Revenue Fund, towards making good any sums which may be appropriated by Parliament, for the payment of expenses in connection with the office of Harbour Master and for the improvement of the harbour of the port for which he is appointed, all moneys received by him for fees under this Act during such year, after deducting therefrom the sum allowed him as aforesaid for his own remuneration ; and if the moneys received by him for fees in any year amount to a less sum than is so allowed him, then such less sum shall be his remuneration for that year.

"11. Such fees as aforesaid shall not be payable for any ship more than twice in each calendar year (that is, the year commencing on the first day of January and ending on the last of December,) whatever be the number of ports or harbours at which she may arrive or pass through, or the number of times of her so arriving or passing through them, or any of them ; such fees shall be payable by the master of the ship to the Harbour Master, immediately on her entering or arriving at the first and second ports or harbours where there is a Harbour Master, and the collector or principal officer of customs thereat shall not grant any clearance, transire or let-pass to any ship on which they are payable, until the master thereof produces to him a certificate of the payment of such fees, or certificates of the payment of fees under this Act twice within the then present year."

12. The Harbour Master of each port shall keep a _{Book to be kept by Harbour Master, and what it must show.} book in which he shall enter from day to day the name of every ship not exempt from the payment of fees under this Act, entering such port, the name of her master, registered tonnage, the date of her entering the port, and the sum, if any, received by him for his fee on her entering, under this Act ; and such book shall be at all times, during office hours, open and free for inspection by any person, on demand, without fee or reward.

13. The powers and duties of the Harbour Master of _{Powers, &c., of Harbour Master appointed under any for-mer law to cease on appointment of one under this Act for the same port.} any port appointed under any authority other than this Act, shall cease to be exercised by him, from the time when the Harbour Master appointed under this Act shall come into office at such port, and shall then and thereafter become and be vested in such last mentioned Harbour Master and his successors in office, in so far

and in so far only as they shall not be inconsistent with this Act, or any rule or regulation made under it ; and all claims, suits or proceedings for penalties incurred or offences committed against law, rule or regulation respecting such port, may be continued to judgment and execution as if this Act had not been passed ; but all fees and all powers, duties, rules, regulations or provisions of law inconsistent with this Act, or any rule or regulation made under it, by whatsoever authority they may have been given, imposed or made, shall cease, and be of no effect by virtue of such appointment under this Act.

To wi. Provinces and ports and when the forego- ing provi- ions shall apply. Ports excepted. 14. The foregoing provisions of this Act shall apply to the Provinces of Quebec, Ontario, British Columbia, and Prince Edward Island only, and to such ports, and such ports only, in either of the said Provinces, as shall, from time to time, be designated for that purpose by Proclamation, under an Order or Orders of the Governor in Council, except only the ports of Quebec and Montreal, in the Province of Quebec, and of Toronto, in the Province of Ontario, to which the said provisions shall not apply.

15. It shall be the duty of each Harbour Master appointed, either under the Act firstly mentioned or the Act secondly mentioned, to see to and superintend the placing, maintaining and taking up of buoys in the port or harbour for which he is appointed, and to perform such other services and duties connected with such port or harbour as he may be directed to perform by the Minister of Marine and Fisheries, or by the proper officer, or by Departmental orders of that department, without any additional remuneration beyond the amount allowed him out of fees received by him under either of the said Acts as hereby amended.

16. The penalty imposed by any rule or regulation made by the Governor in Council, under the fourth section of either of the said Acts, and incurred by any breach or continuing breach of such rule or regulation, may be recovered by summary proceeding and conviction before any Justice of the Peace having jurisdiction in the place where such breach is committed or is continued, under the "Act respecting the duties of Justices of the Peace, out of Sessions, in relation to summary convictions and Orders," on the information of any Harbour Master or other person ; and payment thereof may be enforced in the manner by the said Act provided ; and one moiety of

such penalty shall belong to the informer, not being the Harbour Master, and the other moiety to the Crown ; but if the Harbour Master be the informer, the whole shall belong to the Crown.

RULES AND REGULATIONS FOR THE GOVERNMENT OF CERTAIN PORTS

In the Provinces of

NOVA SCOTIA, NEW BRUNSWICK, QUEBEC, ONTARIO, BRITISH COLUMBIA, AND PRINCE EDWARD ISLAND,

To which the Acts 36 Vic.. Chap. 9, and 37 Vic., Chap. 34, apply; and for the government of the office of Harbour Master for the said Ports.

RULE I.—The following Rules and Regulations shall apply to each and every Port which has been or hereafter may be proclaimed by an Order of the Governor in Council under the provisions of the above named Acts, intituled respectively, "An Act "to provide for the appointment of Harbour Masters for certain " Ports in the Provinces of Nova Scotia and New Brunswick," and " An Act to provide for the appointment of Harbour Masters for "certain Ports in the Provinces of Quebec, Ontario, British Col- "umbia, and Prince Edward Island," unless and until other Rules and Regulations be authorized in such Order or subsequent Order in Council.

RULE II.—It shall be the duty of each Harbour Master of the said Ports, in person or by deputy duly authorized, to go on board of every ship or vessel of the burthen of twenty tons (registered tonnage) and upwards which shall arrive within the said Ports within twelve hours after the arrival of such ship or vessel, to see that she is moored only in such a manner or position as shall be assigned to her by the following Regulations. And it shall be lawful for such Harbour Master to ask, demand and receive, as a compensation for his services (vessels belonging to or employed by Her Majesty and the Government of the Dominion of Canada, and ships engaged in trading between Ports and places in the Dominion, or in the fishing trade, excepted) according to the following scale, and under the restrictions mentioned in the above named Acts :

SCALE OF FEES.

For every ship or vessel of 20 tons, but not more than 80 tons (registered tonnage), 50 cents.

For every ship of 80 tons, but not more than 200 tons, (registered tonnage), $1.00.

For every ship of more than 200 tons, but not more than 300 tons, (registered tonnage), $2.00.

For every ship of more than 300 tons, but not more than 400 tons, (registered tonnage), $3.00.

For every ship of more than 400 tons, $4.00.

RULE III.—In case of any dispute arising between masters, owners or other persons engaged in hauling ships or vessels in or out of any of the docks or wharves, it shall be the duty of the Harbour Master, if called upon, to give such directions as he may think fit in respect to the same ; and all masters, pilots, or other persons having the charge or command of any ships or vessels, shall comply with the directions of the Harbour Master or his deputy in these respects, under the penalty of twenty dollars for each and every neglect or refusal so to do.

RULE IV.—If any ship or vessel arriving and anchoring, or being moored or fastened to any wharf or vessel in the harbour shall be so moored or placed as to be unsafe or dangerous to any other ship or vessel previously lying at anchor in the harbour, or moored or fastened as aforesaid, the Harbour Master or his deputy is hereby authorized and required to forthwith order and direct the situation of such ship or vessel so arriving and anchored, moored or fastened as aforesaid, to be altered in such a manner as to prevent such insecurity and danger; and the master, pilot or other person having charge of such ship or vessel shall comply with the orders and directions of the Harbour Master or his deputy in this respect, under the penalty of twenty dollars for each and every offen. .

RULE V.—Any person or persons who may moor or fasten to, or in any manner injure, alter or change any of the public buoys, shall, on conviction, pay a penalty of twenty dollars, besides being held liable to pay any damage sustained.

RULE VI.—Whenever it shall happen that any ship or vessel is short of hands, so that she cannot be moved when ordered, it shall and may be lawful for the Harbour Master to employ a sufficient number of hands to effect such removal, and to remove or assist in removing such vessel as required or as may be necessary—and that at the expense of such vessel.

RULE VII.—The Harbour master shall have power to order the removal of any scow, boat or other vessel, loaded or unloaded, or anything calculated to interfere with the moving or mooring of vessels from any part of the harbour to any other part thereof, and the owner of such scow, boat, etc., or person in charge thereof, failing to make such removal in one hour after being notified so to do, shall forfeit and pay a sum not exceeding $10, nor less than

$5, and after one hour shall have elapsed the Harbour Master shall have power to make the removal and charge the person notified for so doing.

RULE VIII.—Whenever the Harbour Master shall find ships or vessels at the wharves with main jib or spanker booms rigged out so as to incommode other vessels, it shall be the duty of the Harbour Master to direct such to be rigged in, and in the event of non-compliance, all accidents to the same shall be at the risk of the persons so offending.

RULE IX.—No vessel shall be left without some person to take care of her, by night and by day, when anchored in the stream or in the harbour.

RULE X.—All vessels lying at anchor in the harbour shall keep a clear and bright light burning at least six feet from the uppermost deck, from sunset until sunrise.

RULE XI.—All ships or vessels loading or discharging in the stream, coals, ballast and such like materials, shall have a sufficient piece of canvass or tarpaulin so placed as to prevent any portion thereof from falling into the harbour, under the penalty of $20 for each and every offence, to be paid by the owner, master or person in charge of such ship or vessel.

RULE XII.—No ballast, stone, gravel, earth or rubbish of any kind shall be unladen, cast or emptied out of, or thrown overboard from, any ship or vessel whatever in the harbour, or at the entrance thereof (except in places set apart for that purpose by the Harbour Master and under his direction), under the penalty of fifty dollars for each and every offence, to be paid by the owner, master or other person having the charge of any such ship or vessel.

RULE XIII.—In places set apart by the Harbour Master for the deposit of ballast, etc., it is hereby required that no ballast, stone, gravel, earth or rubbish of any kind shall be unladen, discharged, deposited, thrown or laid before sunrise or after sunset, under a penalty of forty dollars for each and every offence.

RULE XIV.—No ballast, stone, gravel, earth or rubbish of any kind shall be unladen, discharged, deposited, thrown or laid, either from any vessel, boat, scow or other such craft, or in any other manner, or by any person, from any part of the beach or shore into any part of the harbour, or upon the beach or shore thereof, either below low water mark, or between high and low water mark, under the penalty of forty dollars for each and every offence, to be paid by the owner or owners, master or person having charge of any vessel, boat or scow, or other craft from which such matter as aforesaid shall have been discharged, or by any other person or persons violating this law.

44

RULE XV.—Any person or persons who shall or may hinder, oppose, molest or obstruct the Harbour Master, his deputy or any of his assistants in the discharge of his or their duty, shall, on conviction, pay a penalty of forty dollars for each and every offence.

RULE XVI.—The penalty for violation of, or not conforming to the provisions of the law, and for disobeying the lawful orders or directions of the Harbour Master or his deputy in respect to any provision for which no penalty is hereinbefore prescribed, shall be twenty dollars, to be imposed upon the owner or person in charge of the ship or vessel not conforming to the particular requirements.

PRIVY COUNCIL CHAMBER, Ottawa, 3rd December, 1874.

The foregoing Rules and Regulations were submitted to and approved by His Excellency the Governor-General in Council, on the 2nd day of December, instant.

W. A. HIMSWORTH, Clerk Privy Council.

XVIII. WHARVES.

I. The proprietor or occupants of any wharf shall be entitled to the inside berth up to the line of his or their property.

II. The proprietor or occupant of the adjoining property may "overlap" by using the outer berth, or may use the inner berth if not required.

III. Not more than two vessels shall be allowed to lie abreast of any wharf at the same time unless they can do so without occupying a greater depth (or space) than 60 feet from the water front.

The foregoing By-Laws, Rules and Regulations were submitted to and approved by the members present at the Quarterly General Meeting held on the 22d February, and finally adopted at an adjourned General meeting on the 28th February, A. D. 1883.

The Acts of Canada as printed also endorsed.

EBENEZER BROWN, President.

JAMES CUNNINGHAM, Vice-President.

THOMAS J. TRAPP, Secretary.

NEW WESTMINSTER, B. C., 2.h February, 1883.